I0475847

THE GREAT UNRAVEL
Profiting from a transformation in fixed income

By Marilyn Cohen and Chris Malburg

Also by Marilyn Cohen and Chris Malburg

The Little Bond eBook
Surviving the Bond Bear Market: Bondland's
Nuclear Winter
Bonds Now!
The Bond Bible

* * * *

The Great Unravel

By Marilyn Cohen and **Chris** *Malburg*

Library of Congress Cataloging-in-Publication Data
Cohen, Marilyn and Malburg, Chris
The Great Unravel/ Marilyn Cohen Chris Malburg
ISBN 978-1544193007

1. Bonds. 2. Interest rates. 3. Yield 4. Marilyn Cohen 5. Chris Malburg. 6. Municipal bonds 7. Corporate bonds 8. Bond yield

* * * *

Table of Content

Welcome to The Great Unravel

The status quo is no longer. Wherever you look things in America are changing or soon will be. People often don't deal with change very well. Neither do the institutions that regulate and govern our great country. But eventually they recognize things have changed and they get on board. The bond gods do not shower blessings on these changes. Instead, they shower savvy investors with opportunity. Let's be the first to seize them.

Ever since the US Government bailed out the banks and the rest of the financial markets we've had it pretty good. Interest rates are low. Cheap money paved the way for CEOs to use financial engineering to boost the price of their company's stock. Bond and real estate prices also remain high.

While low interest rates put stocks, bonds, and real estate on an upward trajectory, little money actually seeped into the real economy. Throughout the Obama Administration 2-percent and below GDP growth was the stubborn norm.

Many of us wondered when the financial party would end and what event would pierce this bubble? We found out on November 9, 2016 when Donald Trump won the presidential election. Trump's Administration could be the sea change investors have been looking for.

The Great Unravel is a concise look at the key indicators foretelling the changes coming to Bondland and how to profit from them. Certainly the eight years of the Obama Administration created an orgy of zero-percent interest rates. This won't continue. The key questions now facing investors are:

1. Will the US economy reflate with a vengeance?

2. Will infrastructure borrowing by the US Government push the private sector from the capital markets?

3. Will CEOs stop spending on stock buybacks and finally invest in the businesses they're paid to manage?

4. Will President Trump's economic policies grow the economy without causing angry inflation?

5. Will the Bond Vigilantes of the 1980s and 1990s reemerge?

6. Just how dangerous to our financial wellbeing is the public sector's $7 trillion (Moody's estimate) unfunded pension liability?

Each of these questions and their potential solutions will determine whether the bond market completely unravels or gracefully settles into a new trading range.

Key indicators to watch

We professional investors have a number of data points and key indicators we use to gauge the economy. Some actually work for a while. Others identify potential trends. Still others explain what happened and why. Here are five key indicators I watch and what they mean:

Tax reductions

Donald Trump has promised significant tax reductions. These fiscal stimuli for both corporate and personal income tax payers is a welcome change from the tax and spend policies of President Obama. If President Trump is successful in reducing corporate and personal tax rates we could see an increase in the annual growth rate. Alternatively, the effect might be just a one-time increase in the size of the economy that does not affect the future growth rate. Either way the US economy climbs on a higher growth path.

Here's the rub: President Trump portrays himself as a results-oriented manager. What, then, are the anticipated results of a significant tax rate reduction? It depends on how they're financed. Tax cuts financed by immediate cuts in wasteful and nonproductive government spending could raise output. One such program that comes to mind is the $104.5 million spent on building a harbor and an airport in a remote Alaskan town with no roads and just 75 full-time residents.

On the other hand, if tax cuts are financed by reductions in government investment, output falls. Either way, if spending cuts don't accompany tax cuts, there will be an increase in federal borrowing. Should that happen long-term growth may fall.

A tax reduction will grow the economy if its provisions provide a large positive incentive that encourages work, saving, and investment. The tax cuts must be surgical in that they specifically support new economic activity, rather than providing windfall gains for existing sectors. Likewise, a tax reduction package must not distort its effects across economic sectors, different types of income, and consumption. Finally, President Trump will have a far greater likelihood of achieving his growth goal if his tax cut package has minimal effect on the budget deficit.

Housing starts

Find monthly housing start information at https://www.census.gov/construction/nrc/index.html. Around the third week of every month the United States Census Bureau releases to the news media information on new housing starts both nationally and regionally. This information provides the number of new authorized housing units (as counted by building permits).

Various regions of the U.S. have different housing start numbers. That's because certain local economies may be doing better than others and weather patterns may vary. Both issues affect construction.

We believe that housing starts are an important indicator to watch because they reflect so much of the economy. First, builders won't build new houses if they don't think people will buy them. Neither will banks lend to builders if they don't have confidence the economy will absorb these new units, allowing the builders to repay the construction loans.

Strong housing start numbers mean more people will be employed to build houses and apartment buildings. It also foretells an increase in consumer spending as people move into their new homes and purchase durable goods like refrigerators, ovens, washers and dryers as well as sofas and other furniture. The domino effect of increased housing starts on consumer spending is powerful.

Economists see rising housing start numbers as a good sign for the economy. This is not necessarily so for the bond market. We view a string of very strong housing numbers for a 4-6 month period as a sign that the bond market is in for a slide. Here's why. Amid prolonged and soaring housing starts, increased consumer spending and demand raises prices. The bond market soon gets the scent of inflation. Beware, sometimes the bond market is correct; sometimes not.

Credit card delinquencies

Every month the Federal Reserve releases statistics on credit card delinquencies. Consumers make up more than two-thirds of total GDP consumption. If consumers face a credit crunch they'll stop spending. Then GDP cannot grow. Investors holding corporate bonds in consumer cyclical companies would worry about the company's ability to continue servicing their debt.

We view credit card delinquencies as part of the economic domino effect. As always, a single month of change means little. But when at least four months or more move significantly in the same direction we see a trend. For example, a sustained spike in credit card delinquencies may fuel fear that consumer debt is overextended. We begin looking for a recessionary trend in other economic indicators.

Mortgage and car loan delinquencies

Home mortgages and car loans are usually the two largest debt components for most US households. When the delinquency rate of either (or both) trends upward, it is a bad sign for the economy. That's why the Federal Reserve tracks them and periodically reports their change. For delinquent home mortgages, we see a decided downward trajectory since its top in 2010:

Mortgage Delinquencies 1990-2016

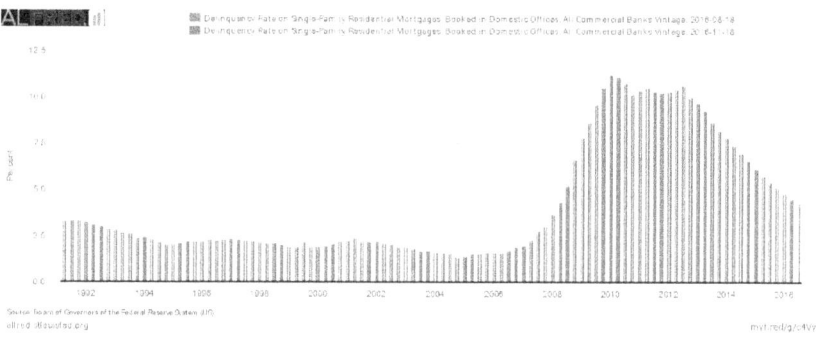

No such good news for delinquent auto loans. Recall the subprime mortgage meltdown that precipitated the 2008 financial crisis. Now we face something similar but with subprime auto loans. No surprise here. Auto lenders are increasingly more aggressive—especially toward people who cannot afford to buy a new car under any circumstances. Car companies and their captive finance units make about half of all car loans. And they underwrite about three-quarters of the auto loans going to subprime vehicle buyers. Subprime auto loan delinquency rates are currently up by double-digit percentages. If you're a car company, this is not what you planned for.

This is such a large component of consumer credit we can't ignore it. Early in 2016 the auto loan bubble topped the one trillion dollar mark ($1.027 trillion between April 1 and June 30, 2016 according to Experian Automotive). The average car loan is now just under $30,000 with monthly payments averaging $499 per car. To put this mountain of debt in perspective, this is enough to buy a new Ford F-150 pickup for every eight or so Americans.

We see this as an indicator of just how fragile our economy is. If the US dips into another recession, the already large number of Americans on the verge of losing their cars to repossession—now 6 million—will swell to record levels. Such an event would have far reaching impacts on the entire debt market. That's why we count mortgage and auto credit delinquencies as a must-watch indicator.

Personal Bankruptcies

We watch the statistics showing movement in personal bankruptcies. A variety of agencies and organizations provide them. One is the American Bankruptcy Institute (www.abi.org). Another is the United States Courts (www.uscourts.gov). Like delinquent car loans, the trend in personal bankruptcies provides insight into how American households are managing their debt.

Events facing fixed income investors

Many wonder if President Trump can make the structural changes our nation and its economy requires. If so, this represents a sea change that will be long lasting. On the other hand, if the promised changes are simply cyclical, they may help for a while, but the US eventually will fade to its old ways.

The Trump administration must overcome three formidable forces: the US is in the most listless expansion since WWII; changing demographics due to baby boomers retiring; and deflationary pressure due to automation. However, if President Trump succeeds in ramping up GDP he will have achieved a singular success he can call his own.

Type of interest rates

You'll hear two different types of interest rates talked about in periods of inflation. The first is the nominal, or stated, interest rate. That's simply the interest rate on a bond without any adjustment for inflation. Some say the nominal interest rate contains the interest rate in a zero inflation environment coupled with investors' demand for added compensation due to inflationary loss of purchasing power. Many economists see the nominal interest rate as an indicator of the market's inflationary expectations. Rising nominal interest rates foreshadow rising inflation; falling nominal rates, predict an expected fall in inflation.

The second type of interest rate is the real interest rate. This the bond interest rate adjusted for inflation. Some see this as a better indicator of an investment portfolio's purchasing power.

Say a bond portfolio has a blended nominal interest rate of 5% and inflation is 2%. The real interest rate of that portfolio is 3%.

Reflating with a vengeance?

Many fixed income investors call inflation the *stealth threat*. That's because it hacks away at the purchasing value of real investment returns. Inflation creates a hurdle the portfolio must clear just to keep real purchasing power even.

Before taking office, the President Elect ignited the so-called Trump Rally in the stock market. This touched off fears that this presidency could usher in a period of rising inflation. As a result bond yields rose as bond prices fell.

No wonder. Mr. Trump promised tax cuts, regulatory rollbacks, and infrastructure spending. The inflationistas agree that all three promises will boost economic growth. But there's a caution to consider. With that positive effect also comes the potential for rising inflation. Recall that these fear-mongers have been wrong before. Most recently was in 2010 when then-Federal Reserve Chairman, Ben Bernanke, undertook a program of monetary stimulus. Since 2012, inflation has not reached the Fed's 2% annual target.

The coming years may indeed bring inflation. But it's the magnitude of inflation that's important. We don't think it will be the 1981 type of hyperinflation. Instead we see the coming inflation as far more muted.

No rampant inflation

We believe the fear of inflationary consequences for such stimulus strategies has been completely discredited. Why? Because the demographics have changed. Inflation has a much different impact on the economic growth of our aging baby boomer population. There isn't as much spending on new homes, cars, gadgets, and vacations. Instead boomers allocate more of their disposable income to healthcare.

Indeed as we write this, the economic forecasting firm, Tradeweb, predicts inflation will climb to 1.88% annually during the next ten years. This is up from their earlier estimate of 1.4%.

We believe the prospect of inflation hinges on US debt. As of December 2016 US debt stands at $19.8 trillion. The Trump Administration has promised a number of stimulus projects America desperately needs. Our roads, rails, and bridges are examples of this necessary overhaul. At the same time there is a promised corporate tax cut. Barring other countering programs, it seems US debt will rise, but not necessarily like it did under the last administration.

However, this may not actually kick up inflation as some expect. Let's continue with the road and rail improvement idea. Back in the 1930s with the New Deal, then again in the 1950s when the highway construction spending program we discovered the benefits of efficient transportation. Costs actually fell, keeping prices in check. Runaway inflation never happened. We could see the same thing under President Trump's infrastructure restoration plan. It all depends on how the infrastructure plan is financed.

Don't forget the market factors that influence inflation. Rising interest rates and a stronger dollar may restrain the economy, thus putting the brakes on inflation. We believe inflation will rise, but in a controlled posture that does not put the bond market on its back.

Investment strategies for moderate inflation

Some of Envision Capital's clients have expressed a fear of unleashed inflation. For them, we're moving a portion of their holdings into securities designed to counteract inflation. Here's the mechanics of our strategy:

1. We're buying corporate bonds with a fixed rate plus a CPI floating component.

2. We're allocating a portion of the portfolios to floating-rate notes whose coupons rise and fall with Treasurys or the London Interbank Offered Rate (LIBOR). These move in the same direction as does inflation—though the correlation is admittedly imperfect.

3. Some Investors want Treasury inflation protected securities (TIPS). These are indexed to inflation to counteract the negative effects on purchasing power.

4. Variable rate bonds are another way to reduce the negative effects of moderate inflation. We're buying 3-month LIBOR floaters with a decent fixed rate.

Our last strategy for dealing with moderate inflation has to do with our overall investment strategy. Envision Capital rarely, if ever, buys bond funds. And we certainly don't buy bond funds in an inflationary environment unless they are hedged. The reason is that you'll lose less to eroding bond prices due to inflation by buying the individual bonds. Bond funds, on the other hand, will experience a mass exodus once the market gets a whiff of inflationary expectations. When that happens redemptions in the fund will work against investors trying sell their fund holdings. More on hedged ETFs and funds later.

What if interest rates spike?

US interest rates began climbing after Brexit in July. Their rise gained momentum after the US presidential election in November. Further, the Federal Reserve said it expects three policy-rate hikes in 2017. So, yes rates are going higher. Will they spike? Will the bond market be ahead of the Fed as usual?

We don't think so. Yet this is a fear of so many fixed income investors. Our philosophy is to plan for the worst and hope for the best. We definitely have a strategy for dealing with spiking interest rates.

Duration

Managing a bond portfolio's exposure to interest rate fluctuations has everything to do with that portfolio's duration. Let's put duration in perspective: First, duration is a complex calculation involving present value, yield, coupon, final maturity and call features. You won't ever have to calculate it yourself. Duration is a standard data point provided by most every bond fund and ETF we know of. The industry expresses duration as a number. It is not years; just a number. The bigger the duration, the greater the interest-rate risk for portfolios.

For example, say a bond portfolio has a duration of 10. This means that for every 1% rise in interest rates, that bond portfolio will lose 10% of its value. Likewise, a bond portfolio with a duration of, say 2, will lose just 2% of its value for every 1% rise in interest rates.

The takeaway here is that if you believe interest rates are going to spike or even steadily rise, you want a short duration bond portfolio. You can manage the duration of your bond portfolio by loading it with near term maturing bonds. The shorter the maturities of your bond portfolio, the shorter its duration.

What the pros are doing

Professional investors need a way to manage the duration of their bond portfolios. Using ETFs to lower duration seems to be a favorite tool. Short-term debt ETFs took in over $5 billion in the three months between November 2016 and January 2017. Similarly, senior loan ETFs received $1.7 billion and floating-rate debt ETFs added $1.1 billion over the same time period.

Hedging with ETFs

ETFs give us the ability to manage our portfolio's exposure to both interest rate fluctuations as well as particular market segments. It's a strategic 2-for-1 solution to a worrisome problem for anxiety-ridden investors.

Here's a good example of how it works. The ProShares Investment Grade Interest Rate Hedged ETF (IGHG) takes a long position in its corporate bond portfolio with a concurrent duration-matched position in US Treasury futures. This particular ETF then provides investors with exposure to high-grade corporate bonds with a hedge against rising interest rates.

Two other similar rate-hedged investment grade ETFs are: iShares Interest Rate Hedged Corporate Bond ETF (LQDH) and Deutsche X-Trackers Investment Grade Interest Rate Hedged ETF (IGIH).

Another ETF that has enjoyed a 1000% moon shot increase in assets since the November elections is BlackRock's Rate-Hedged Junk ETF (HYGH). Like the previous ProShares ETF, HYGH investors are hedging against rising yields (falling bond prices) and expected interest rate hikes with a junk bond portfolio. In this case HYGH shorts Treasury futures and targets a duration of zero. This means that interest rate rises will not impact the ETF. HYGH assets from 2016 have gone from $21 million to $208 million in early 2017.

See how these two ETFs work? One allows investors to take a position in investment grade bonds; the other, in junk bonds. Both provide a hedge against rising interest rates and sport good yields in their sectors.

Floating rate notes ETFs

We like floaters. They ratchet up payment as interest rates rise. Investors have caught on to buying Floating Rate Notes ETFs to spread the risk of rising rates. Since the component notes in these ETFs reset when market interest rates change, their prices fluctuate less than individual bonds with similar maturities.

One example of a quality floating rate note ETF is the iShares Floating Rate Bond ETF (FLOT). This ETF uses corporate high grade floating paper in its portfolio.

The number of Floating Rate ETS is increasing. Just one example is the SPDR Barclays Investment Grade Floating Rate ETF (FLRN). This ETF tracks the Barclays U.S. Dollar Floating Rate Note < 5 Years Index. Its average maturity as of this writing was 1.73 years with a duration of 0.12. The sectors this ETF tracks are composed of 61% financial sector holdings followed by the industrial sector with 25%.

Our recommendations

If you wish to put on a hedge against rising (or spiking) interest rates, here are three ETFs we like:

1. iShares Interest Rate Hedge ETF (HYGH): This ETF is a fund of funds holding high yield corporate

bonds with short positions in US Treasury futures. It has a good yield and excellent liquidity ($208 million) making for easy entry and exit.

2. ProShares High Yield Interest Rate Hedged ETF (HYHG): Similar to the iShares ETF. It provides a good yield, but less liquidity (around $100 million) than the iShares.

3. iShares Interest Rate Hedged Corporate Bond ETF (LQDH): Holds corporate bonds and hedges interest rates by shorting US Treasury futures. Its expense ratio is good—just .25%. However, its volume is just $47 million. We put this on our watch list and recommend purchase if its total assets ever climb above $100 million.

Government crowding out

Crowding out is the term economists use when public sector spending or borrowing drives down private sector spending or debt issuance. Some say crowding out has the effect of raising interest rates. It's a question that now haunts professional money managers and individual investors alike. President Trump has an ambitious list of projects: Rebuilding the nation's infrastructure, reducing the burden of government regulations, trade deficit reduction, tax code overhaul, increased domestic energy production, the list goes on. For those that are capital intensive, where will the money come from?

The business as usual answer is Treasury debt. According to some, such a ramp-up in government issued debt of the magnitude required could discourage private enterprise from engaging in infrastructure projects.

Here's how crowding out works: Let's say a manufacturing company plans on building a new production line in its factory. The new line costs $5 million and will return $6 million. Loans to the company are at 3%. Net income on the project is $1 million.

However, at the same time the government announces a large stimulus package that will help businesses but will also raise the interest rate on new loans. Suddenly the interest rate our manufacturing company pays on its loans rises to 4%—a 33% increase. Our company must now spend $5.75 million on the project to return the same $6 million. The company's projected earnings just sank from $1 million to $250,000—a 75% drop. They were just crowded out of the debt market. They cancel the new production line.

This is not business as usual

Economists make a good case for rising interest rates as the private sector is crowded out of the debt markets by new government borrowing. However, we believe President Trump and his team of experienced business professionals are smarter than that. He's already shown how he thinks out of the box. The vast fiscal stimulus programs he has promised along with a corporate tax cut will raise US debt over its current $20 trillion if he financed it using traditional instruments. US Treasurys, to be precise.

Instead, we believe the government will steer clear of Treasurys—the Obama Administration's primary financing vehicle. The new administration is no longer composed of theoreticians, academics, and bureaucrats who never had to make payroll. The new guard is composed of street-smart, practical business people who actually have to produce results. They are inventive, adaptive, and have a mandate to solve America's problems quickly.

We think the US government will—at least in part—pay for this new round of spending and tax cuts by issuing 50 and 100-year Treasury bonds. They will also make use of tax credits, private partnerships, and the taxable municipal bond market. There is also the possibility that a *US Infrastructure Fund* could be created. The USIF then would issue the debt and the US government would guarantee it.

Who would buy such ultra-long term bonds? Probably not individual investors. Most likely the buyers would be public and private pension managers with an actuarial mandate to match fund demands with income and maturity schedules.

None of these *business as unusual* financing methods will compete with the private sector. There will be no crowding out and a lesser likelihood of an increase in interest rates. We believe that this is the US economy's reset moment. President Obama proved that monetary stimulus failed. For eight torturous years our economy languished at a 2 percent or less growth rate. It's time to give fiscal stimulus a chance.

Investment strategies for infrastructure spending

If we're wrong about President Trump's spending plan not crowding out the private sector and other governmental borrowers from the debt market, then interest rates will rise more than anticipated and a traditional bond strategy won't work. However, we believe rates will not see a substantial rise. Therefore our investment strategy includes:

1. Maintain short duration bond portfolios

2. Over allocate—say 15%-20% of the portfolio—to flexible instruments such as CPI corporate floaters, hedged floating rate ETFs, and floating rate bank loan funds.

The most useful indicators

We have several indicators that show us how the bond market is behaving. Movement by a single one of these indicators means little. However, a sustained trend over several months along with a similar move in a complimentary indicator catches our attention.

When we're tracking demand for US bonds the two most useful indicators we've found are the bid to cover ratio and the TIC figure. Here's how they work and what they mean:

Bid to cover ratio

The bid to cover shows demand present at US Treasury bond auctions. Essentially it tracks the number of bond buyers compared to bond availability. A bid to cover ratio of 2.0 means there were twice as many bidders as there were bonds to sell. Conversely, a falling ratio means fewer bidders showed up for the bond auction. This could foretell a condition of crowding out.

The TIC figure

The full name for the TIC is the Treasury International Capital figure. It reports the net transactions by foreign investors in US securities. The TIC also tells foreign demand for US securities and the demand for US dollars needed to purchase those securities. A fall in the TIC figure often foretells a weakening dollar. A weakening dollar can mean greater export activity by the US.

As with most economic indicators, the trend is what's important. If we see the TIC figure falling over several months we know global investors are staying away from the US Treasury bond market.

What? Me invest in the business?

Yes. You, Mr. CEO. It's what all bond investors want to see their bond issuers do. Will they start investing in their business or will they keep spending the company's precious cash and cash flow on stock buybacks to line the executive's performance based pockets? Borrowing to invest in the business can make a solid and sustainable return on investment. Say the money goes to machinery and equipment or capital projects that allows the company to enter a new market. It actually adds to long-term shareholder value.

Borrowing to buy back the company's own stock, on the other hand, offers only illusory value to shareholders. It is a short-term remedy designed to line the executive's pockets whose compensation is paid partly in stock options and other stock appreciation contrivances. The stock may rise in the near term—just long enough for the senior execs and board to exercise their stock options—but will eventually fall again for exactly the same reasons it was down in the first place.

However, the debt incurred to fund the stock buyback will be there for years to come.

As bond investors, we want to see improvement in an issuer's ability to cover its debts and to increase free cash flow (used to repay we bond investors). Incurring debt to buy back the company's own stock serves neither purpose. But borrowing for capital projects does improve the company. Finally, as financial engineering debt declines and is replaced with capital projects expenditures the US GDP grows.

Now there are a number of possibilities for corporations to amass their cash and invest it back into the company. Consider President Trump's plan to repatriate profits held hostage by US corporations in foreign countries with lower corporate tax rates. The enticement for corporations to bring their treasure back to American shores is the slashed corporate tax rate from 35% to 15%. If that occurs, the US becomes competitive with the rest of the world. They would pay a much smaller slice of their profits made in America. They have more to invest in their companies. Business expands.

Add to that President Trump's moral suasion: It's good business to keep your manufacturing, your people, and your treasure right here in America. It's good to be an American and to support America.

Naturally there will be laws and regulations governing repatriation of this estimated $2 trillion in repatriated profits. However, it's a good start to turning around the CEO's thinking about using organic growth to raise their stock price rather than pursuing the temporary benefits of financial engineering.

As we write this, Carrier's decision not to move part of one manufacturing facility to Mexico is in the headlines. It's a small victory for America, but a victory nevertheless. Carrier and its management team received the kind of positive press that cannot be manufactured by any advertising agency or public relations firm. We can't wait to see what other companies follow suit, how it affects their stock price, and what it does to their bonds.

Effects on the markets

Shortly after the election the bond market suffered a stunning selloff. Those bondholders who focused on the short term saw their portfolio value decline as yields jumped.

However, for the fixed income investors who own bonds for the income they produce over time there is a silver lining when yields rise. This increases the income bondholders can expect from new purchases. Those with short duration portfolios will be trading in those low yielding bonds maturing in the next few years for higher income producing bonds.

It's a cycle. When bond yields were low, investors bought stocks. Now that bond yields appear to be rising, the same investors who profited from the stock market will rotate into bonds.

One sector in particular that's poised for a reversal of fortune is the financials and the big pension funds. That only makes sense. As interest rates, inflation, and economic growth rise, so does financial income. For financial institutions net interest income—the spread between what banks pay for deposits and what they earn on investments—widens as interest rates rise. According to Bank of America's chief economist, Paul Donofrio, a single percentage point increase in yields across all maturities would lift BofA's net interest income $5.3 billion in the next twelve months.

What to do when/if these things happen

No matter if you've been an active investor or sat on the sidelines, now is the time to act. If inflation ramps up, government spending does the same, and if bond yields climb, here is what we are putting our clients in and what we recommend:

1. LIBOR floating rate notes that include a fixed component that's as high as possible

2. Inverse exchange traded funds (ETF). There is a caution with these: The timing of any rate hike must be right or

they won't help control the damage of an unraveling bond market.

3. Variable rate bonds or ETFs with floating rates hedged or unhedged

4. Short duration fixed-coupon bonds

5. Inflation adjusted CPI bonds

Additionally, we always pay close attention to the portfolio composition. Allocation is important in managing inflationary effects. The more rapid inflation and the increase in governmental spending the greater we believe should be your allocation to rate adjusting instruments. These counter inflation's negative effects and take advantage of climbing bond rates.

Will the Bond Vigilantes emerge?

Economist, media pundit, and financial seer, Ed Yardeni, was first to call them Bond Vigilantes in the 1980's. These are institutional investors who own enormous bond positions. They short the bonds of issuers they don't like. These are sometimes governments with unsustainable fiscal policies. They also short corporate and municipal bonds for the same reasons. Then they wait for the issuer to run into fiscal disaster. Another scenario is that interest rates on the target bonds rise so high that they can't roll over their debt. Bond values plummet and the vigilantes close out their short positions. They clean up. Then they search out the next issuer to hose.

When acting together, these institutional bond vigilantes can short a particular issuer *en masse*. This action erodes investor confidence and creates a tumultuous bond market. Everything falls as a result.

Watch the media for word of the bond vigilantes and their activities. You will see massive selling in particular bonds— like they did with Greece and with British Petroleum bonds during the Gulf Coast disaster like they did with all energy bonds in 2016. The vigilantes have the power to force governments and corporations to change policy more to their liking. Bond vigilante actions can come suddenly. Their effects can be devastating both to issuers and to the bond market.

The China factor

China and the other Asian Tigers lead the world's economy. The US relies on China to buy its Treasurys. That is how we finance our massive debt and budget deficits. The fact is, one day China will no longer need to buy foreign investments such as US Treasurys. A more beneficial and profitable investment of their Yuan will be found in their own economy.

When that occurs, China will slow their buying of Treasurys or—worst case—boycott the auctions entirely. The US needs Japan and China (the second biggest Treasury buyer) as we roll over our Treasury debt. Without robust demand for US Treasurys we have no visible means of keeping this debt balloon aloft.

China has made it clear that they do not approve of the US' massive debt. We aren't sure the US government is listening. Witness the US Congress drafting a resolution asking China to please not manipulate their currency to the US' detriment. This single act humiliated China on the world's financial stage. It demonstrated just how fiscally ignorant our leaders really are.

As the number one buyer of US Treasurys, Japan and China are in the position to exert enormous economic force on the US government if they so choose. If that turns into vigilante behavior, it will detonate a nuclear explosion in the bond market.

So far China just seems worried about the stability of its bond issuer—the United States. However, China will eventually decide it no longer needs to recycle its trade balance surpluses into US Treasury securities. This occurs when:

- China turns to buying domestic rather than foreign. This leaves discretionary investment funds in-country rather than sending them to the US.

- Domestic consumption drives China's economy

- China's middle class can finally afford homes, apartments, cars and consumer goods and services. This makes exports less important

- China starts producing its own consumer items internally in ever-increasing quantities. Quality rivals or exceeds that of any producer the world over.

- Should China reduce its purchase of US Treasurys the US will have to pedal its Treasurys elsewhere— at much higher rates.

Unfunded pensions

These relate to municipalities that issue bonds. We bondholders carefully watch just how these issuers' unfunded pension obligations grow. Some will astound you. The question becomes just how dangerous to our financial wellbeing is the public sector's unfunded pension liability? In our strategic thinking, it is very dangerous. Unfunded pensions represent a looming liability—$2 trillion nationwide as of this writing. It will have to be paid some day. That someday is getting closer and closer.

One fear every sophisticated bondholder has is what happens to their bonds if the municipality that issued them goes or needs to restructure its debt? This is a horrible proposition for many bondholders. One example is the City of Detroit that underwent a Chapter 9 bankruptcy in 2014. Like so many before and since, the pensioners came out far better than the bondholders. That's because the bondholders do not live there and are not voters. Those running the municipality want to appease its constituents—the pensioners. There's no political fallout for local elected officials negotiating the bankruptcy settlement. They can and do stick it to the bondholders with total immunity. Afterall, the bondholders are not voters in the district.

Detroit pushed water and sewer bondholders to make sacrifices (politico-speak for forcing bondholders to take a haircut on their debt). This, even though the water and sewer bonds were guaranteed by the city's utility, which wasn't even in bankruptcy and had been paying its debt on time.

The city also forced bondholders who held debt tied to property taxes to take less than they were owed. This too was a surprise. Bonds paid with property tax revenue had never been subject to a haircut. The stories of Detroit and Stockton illustrate how local leaders predictably push plans that favor public workers (voters) over bondholders. In all, those holding Detroit bonds came away with pennies on the dollar while the pensions faired much better, taking just a 20% haircut in benefits.

Dallas' unfunded pension fund

Dallas is a glittering city—full of construction and all the signs of membership in America's fastest growing 13 largest cities. However, there's a problem that threatens to take the Big D under. That is the near collapse of the city's pension fund for its police officers and firefighters.

During six weeks in late 2016 panicked Dallas police and fire pensioners yanked $220 million out of the fund. The reason? First came reports that the fund's investments were both risky and highly speculative. Then it was disclosed that these questionable investments were worth a fraction of their cost. Second was a proposal that retirees no longer be allowed to talk out big blocks of money from the fund.

Even an infusion of $1.1 billion would not come close to bridging Dallas' unfunded pension gap. This number did not come from thin air. It is the amount of Dallas' general fund budget for the entire year. It puts in perspective how fiscally desperate the city is and highlights the fact that there is no way out.

What caused Dallas' enormous unfunded pension gap (currently estimated at $7 billion)? In Dallas' case that was a target return of 9% in a 2% market. Investment managers began taking more and more risk to come close to the 9% goal. Such desperate strategies never work in investors' favor.

Back in 1993 Texas lawmakers gave the police and firefighters a most extraordinary pension package: Pension payouts beyond anyone's wildest dreams; individual savings accounts paying 8.5% annually; and a retirement age with full benefits of 50.

We wish we could say that Dallas is not that much different than other cities around America with huge unfunded pension liabilities. Most have come about due to unrealistic payout deals for city workers. Almost all have investment return assumptions way above what their managers can actually produce.

Aiding and abetting fiscal dysfunction

There is a conga line of municipalities on the edge of default. And they're not all cities. Along with Atlantic City, there is Illinois—which some see as the next Detroit. What are the signs investors should look for? The answer is simpler than you think:

1. Read the financial news: Bloomberg, *The Wall Street Journal, Barron's*
2. Look at the numbers—specifically unfunded pension liabilities
3. Act: Take action no matter how painful and sell those municipal bonds that seem in peril

Take Atlantic City for example: Its 12 casinos once comprised 70% of the city's property tax base. Today just eight of those casinos are still open, three of which are operating in bankruptcy. Competition for gambling dollars is fierce. Atlantic City's casino revenue in 2006 was $5.2 billion. By 2014 it had fallen to just $2.5 billion. The city is deeply in debt. According to Bloomberg News, Atlantic City has borrowed $345 million since 2010. This money went to plug municipal deficits and tax appeals. Debt service—the money needed to repay principal keep current on interest—now accounts for a whopping 15% of Atlantic City's budget. All this has caused Moody's to downgrade Atlantic City's general obligation debt from Ba1 to Caa1—a high risk of default over the next five years.

Governor Christie issued an executive order and assembled an emergency management and turnaround team. Guess who was the special consultant advising on this undertaking? Drum roll…it was Kevin Orr. Yes, the very same Kevin Orr who put

Detroit into bankruptcy. We're reminded of the saying, *when all you have is hammer, everything looks like a nail.* Should Orr's advice result in Atlantic City filing for bankruptcy, bondholders will surely get the short end of the stick—again.

Atlantic City's cash is dwindling. Pension payment obligations are piling up. Things look grim for Atlantic City. Price and yield on their bonds tell the story: Atlantic City New Jersey General obligation bonds maturing Feb. 2020 yield 5.70%. Consider it a bad omen.

Following right behind Detroit and Atlantic City in the fiscal dysfunction category are Illinois (yes, the entire state), Chicago, Puerto Rico, and the Virgin Islands.

California Highway Patrol

The California Highway Patrol is among the finest law enforcement agencies to be found anywhere. It is composed of committed men and women who do a marvelous job. Problem is they want to be paid for their work. Imagine such a demand. The California Public Employees Retirement System manages the CHP's pension fund. They have consistently underperformed against their target ROI.

However, that's just the beginning of the problem out in California. Back in the Dot.com era, the State decided to boost benefits to the CHP's pension package. The managers assumed the Internet stock bubble and the market gains the pension fund would reap could pay for it. They reduced the pensioner retirement age to 50 and gave them a greater percentage of their salaries. No question the fine CHP officers deserved it. But this decision had enormous ramifications to the Fund's financial stability. When the Dot.com bubble burst the pension fund's ROI simply could not catch up with demands from its members to pay out the retirement money they were promised. Add to that people are living longer. For the last decade the number of CHP pension beneficiaries have outnumbered active members. This is a financial hole with seemingly no bottom.

In 2017 California Governor Jerry Brown decided to levy a tax to pay for the CHP's pension shortfall. He added $10 to vehicle registration fees. This money doesn't go toward keeping

California's roads and highways in drivable condition. It goes exclusively to the CHP's pension fund.

One other thing happened. Calpers—the fund investment manager—lowered the investment return target by just a half percentage point to 7% for the next three years. This is a political hot potato because it now requires the state and its municipalities to make even larger pension contributions. If they can't or just won't, then the pension fund will fall that much further behind. As if that weren't enough, there are some who say that 7% ROI target is still too high and unrealistic. Either way you look at it, the CHP pension fund is in a heap of trouble.

Kicking the can down the road

So many municipal issuers have been derelict in funding their pension obligations. When they have a budget shortfall, they just decide to short change the full pension fund contribution. It has happened so often for so long that many elected officials treat pension contributions as a discretionary expenditure. The year it happens, no one complains. There's still plenty of money in the fund to pay *that year's* obligations. By the time anyone figures out the trouble the municipality is in, the officials responsible will be long gone anyway. This is what's called kicking the can down the road.

The real danger

Public pensions are built on assumptions. The first is when will those eligible for pension fund payout retire and begin drawing their promised money. The rule for early retirement by employees who want to be sure they get their share is: First in, most out. We saw that with Dallas Police & Fire Pension. The second is how much money were they promised? And third, what is the return on investment the fund must achieve to meet the payout demands?

Taking these one at a time, the first question is when? When can the fund expect its beneficiaries to retire and begin drawing their money? This is actuarially determined. It's a science based on mathematics and statistics. However, for some pension funds (such as Dallas) the politicians stepped in and adjusted the retirement age. When that happens—especially when they reduce the retirement age—actuarial assumptions are no longer valid. There's going to be a much larger draw and far earlier than expected.

The second question—how much was promised—is equally devastating. When municipal leaders raise pension benefits of the fund participants (most probably voters) the pool of available funds to pay out circles the drain faster. Usually faster than anyone thought.

Finally comes the return on the fund's investments. This is a number that seems a work of fiction for so many pension funds. Pension managers pushed their ROI assumptions sky high in order for their bosses to justify cutting the annual pension contribution. Had they not done that, then the pension funds would have hired a manager who would do it. The theory was that they could make up the contribution shortfall in future years with greater ROI contributions.

Now the chickens have come home to roost. In many cases the pension fund ROI assumptions are anywhere between two and four *times* what the market will bear. For every year the pension investment managers fail to achieve their target return and the municipality shorts their pension contribution, the funds get further and further behind. It is like a negative compounding on a credit card that's never paid off but continues to be used.

Pension Obligation Bonds

These are bonds issued by a state or municipality with unmanageable unfunded pension liabilities. The theory behind POBs is that the pension managers (who have already failed once to meet their investment target) can invest the bond proceeds at a higher rate than the bond coupon paid to the bondholders and pay the profit back into the pension fund to reduce the unfunded liability.

According to the Government Finance Officers Association this creates an enormous risk for the POB issuer. What happens if the pension manager fails to make a profit investing the bond proceeds? Now the fund has dug an even deeper hole for itself. In another scenario, what happens if the municipality decides to take the POB proceeds and use them to pay for other operating expenses? Some may say that this could not happen; that the POB proceeds are ring-fenced against such an occurrence. Still, we've seen some strange things in our 30 years in this business.

Beware of the De Minimis rule

When individuals invest in municipal bonds they expect 100% tax-free income. Right? Well, many may unknowingly be setting themselves up for a tax bill from the IRS. How can this be? Afterall we're talking munis.

It's been many years since the municipal bond De Minimis rule was relevant. Now, as interest rates are poised to rise, bond prices will fall. Investors are more likely to buy bonds at a discount. We believe the Machiavellian tax code designed the De Minimis rule for just such and event.

The reason we have not been plagued until recently with the De Minimis rule is that issuers weren't issuing many 2%, 2.25%, 2.50%, or 3% municipal bonds until 2016 when yields touched such low levels. Then post election, muni yields rose and prices declined wickedly.

Here's how the rule works in plain English: Say you purchase a low coupon municipal bond for a 2%, 2.25%, 2.50%, or even 3% coupon at a discount from its face value in the secondary market. If that discount breaches the IRS De Minimis threshold, then a portion of that discount can be taxed as ordinary income and/or a portion as capital gains.

It all depends on how deeply the bond price is discounted. The simple formula to compute the De Minimis threshold is:

> De Minimis threshold = Lower of par or original issue discount – (.25% X the years to maturity)

If this sounds like IRS gobbly-gook you are right. The law prevents taxpayers from converting ordinary income into capital gains. Remember the only IRS rule you should commit to memory is, *Whatever is best for the government and worst for the taxpayer is the correct rule interpretation.*

26

Here's an example. Assume you purchased 50 XYZ Unified School District municipals, 2.00% coupon maturing September 1, 2028 originally issued at par, 100. If you purchased the bonds in the secondary market today at 90.288 for a 3.00% Yield to Maturity because rates rose since issuance, you will owe $2107.50 in tax on $50,000 face value of the bonds.

The market discount cutoff price was 97.25. Any discount below that threshold is taxed. Okay—paying $2107.50 in tax on 50 munis isn't the end of the world. Still, it could blindside you if your weren't aware of the De Minimis rule.

How to avoid the De Minimis rule

If you want all your return to be tax-free then invest in higher coupon bonds at par or a slight premium. Stay away from market discounted munis. If you're doing business with a retail broker ask them to run the analytics on Bloomberg. That will quickly compute your tax liability if purchasing at a discounted price.

One caution: If interest rates rise significantly, high coupon premium bonds can decline and breach the De Minimis threshold too.

The De Minimis rule also has a significant impact on your bond price. Should you decide to sell a bond subject to the De Minimis rule your sale of the bond will be at an even deeper discount. The buyer will demand compensation for that portion of their [now] taxable return.

If you buy munis online and your platform does not supply a De Minimis calculator better get out your pencil and paper for hand computations. There are numerous articles online written by Piper Jaffray, Pimco, Schwab, RBC and others explaining the formulas and with grids showing allowable market discounts before treatment as ordinary income kicks in.

The De Minimis rule can bite careless investors. Oh…and if you think no one will notice the discounted price you paid, the 1099s issued by the brokerage industry are extremely accurate in their reporting to the IRS.

Productivity

Economists at General Electric estimate that if the world boosted industrial productivity by just 1 percent, it could add *$15 trillion* to the global gross domestic product over the next 15 years. That's quite a forecast. Whether the boys at GE are right in their numbers it is true that productivity drives the economy.

With President Trump's new economic goals America might well experience a swing from mere financial engineering intended only to temporarily raise a company's stock price to true capital spending that actually strengthens our country's businesses. Some pundits say this could transition our economy from a service base to a manufacturing base. If true, then productivity of our businesses and workforce must increase for corporate profits to rise.

We believe that America's lack of increased labor productivity over the last eight years is due in part to the expansion of regulatory oversight. If President Trump succeeds in reducing the burdensome regulations now stifling American business that, along with expectations for rising interest rates in 2017, could fuel a new growth in productivity.

Productivity effects on bonds

If there is strong economic growth, then the prospect for stocks and private investment improves. Bonds grow less attractive driving yields up and bond prices down.

Look at the financial sector

The Dodd-Frank bill devastated commercial bank labor productivity. Suddenly absurd amounts of money and employees were deployed for nothing more than governmental compliance work. It did nothing to help the banks deliver their services to customers. Bank labor productivity fell to just 0.3 percent annualized in the 2010s. Compare this to the 3.3 percent productivity in the 2000s and 4.8 percent in the 1990s.

Then came the Volker Rule just one year later in 2011. This pretty much eliminated proprietary trading inside the big banks. The financial industry suffered a double-whammy of regulation.

Then in 2015 the banks again faced regulatory excess, this time in the form of higher capitalization requirements.

Impact on critical services

Along with over regulating America's key industries we see health care providers, educational institutions, and food services as sectors where increases in productivity are practically dormant. Indeed these industries are the ones at the top of President Trump's reform list.

Since growth in productivity largely determines America's living standard President Trump can make his mark by unshackling the US economy from its overburden of government regulations. We believe this could begin a new era of productivity, dynamism, and corporate efficiency.

Pay Attention to the Jobs Report

Of all the economic reports released each month, the jobs report has the largest impact on the bond market. The reason the jobs report is so important is that the job market is the heartbeat of the American economy. It is both an indicator of economic health—since a strong economy prompts companies to hire more workers—and an engine of growth, since higher employment means more dollars available to be spent on goods and services. Without job growth, overall economic growth is likely to be limited no matter what else is happening in other areas of the economy.

A key aspect of the report is not just how many jobs or added or lost, but how the result compares to market expectations. A jobs report that shows 50,000 jobs added in a particular month may not indicate that the economy is roaring, but if expectations were for negative growth, the market typically reacts to the *surprise*, not the absolute number.

Impact of a positive Jobs Report

Investors take a positive jobs report as a sign that economic growth is on track. This depresses bond prices for two reasons: First, it makes the Federal Reserve more likely to raise interest rates in the future. Since the fed funds rate heavily influences yields on short-term bonds, the prospect of the Fed raising rates causes yields to rise and prices to fall for Treasuries and other rate-sensitive segments of the market such as municipal bonds, mortgage-backed securities, and higher-quality corporate bonds.

Second, stronger economic growth raises the likelihood of inflation. Since higher inflation eats away at bond prices, the prospect of rising price pressure is typically a negative for bonds. While the connection between growth and inflation is tenuous and uneven in reality, for the jobs report, it's perception that counts.

Impact of a negative jobs report

The bond market perks up in the face of a negative jobs report. The Fed is more likely to cut interest rates than to increase them. A negative jobs report—or one that doesn't reach expectations—reduces the odds of inflation. Both are positive for the performance of US Treasuries and other rate-sensitive investments.

Wage Increases

Contained in the jobs report is information on wage increases. If President Trump succeeds in raising full time American wages rather than just part time wages, the effect will be similar to an increase in the number of jobs: The stock market will go up, bond yields will also go up and bond prices will fall.

Strategies for productivity and jobs

What's good for America's economy is typically good for the stock market and bad for the bond market. Since Donald Trump's election, sentiment seems to be going in different directions for stocks and bonds. The stock market's implied volatility is down 25%. Bond implied volatility is up 30%. Typically, those indicators are 80% correlated. So we have a disconnect. A decrease in equity volatility makes investors a little more confident. Conversely as bond volatility rises, investors see more risk.

We believe the market is overestimating the number of shovel-ready projects for fiscal spending. If true, this would be a negative for equities and a positive for bonds. On the other hand the markets may be underestimating the huge potentially positive impact of tougher trade restrictions, and less immigration. Both are negatives for economic growth. They would depress the equity market and improve bonds.

There's one more consideration looming on the economic horizon. President Trump has stated that he wants to bring back the $2.4 trillion dollars American corporations have parked overseas. If that's repatriated, and used for capital expenditures, it will be very simulative for the economy as well.

This analysis brings us to our bond strategy for the coming year. Bond investors should consider hedging their bond bets. Add moving parts—floating rate bonds, CPI and LIBOR based securities. This allows you portfolio flexibility. You participate on the upside and don't get nuked if things fall apart.

The paradigm has shifted. The question is, just how much will it shift. We believe the bond market will move into a higher trading range for yields. This means, those investors who keep their duration short, maintain floating rate positions will profit. As their short duration bonds mature, they will reinvest in higher yielding bonds.

Policies over the past eight years forced interest rates down. This increased bond portfolio values. Investors were happy. But they didn't have any more cash flow to spend. You can't spend total return. That's why if rates rise to a higher trading range, investors will enjoy greater cash flow and income to spend or reinvest. As money managers, we look forward to that happening.

Conclusion

The Brexit/Trump victories were about breaking out of the economic stagnation in which Great Britain and America found themselves. Some say the more than 30-year US Bond Bull Market is over. Maybe. But there are lots of buts: But our 2% and sub-2% GDP growth during the last eight years isn't like 1981, 1989, and 1994, all of which brought with them inflation and higher interest rates. Those were wicked, bloody Bond Bear markets that we baby boomers suffered through.

America is moving into a higher trading range for bond yields. We believe that inflation will be muted—perhaps 2-3%. And there will be both economic and revenue growth. This is just what we Boomers and retirees need: higher interest rates to supplement income and improve quality of life.

Just as we saw during the presidential election, the so-called pundits and self-proclaimed media savants who ask us to trust their judgment proved they actually know very little. We witnessed first hand what Dorothy in the *Wizard of Oz* saw behind the curtain—just a talking head with enough makeup to make them appear nice-looking. There was nothing of any substance behind the mask. Our takeaway is that these media darlings babbling about the economy and what drives it have a dismal record of accurately predicting what will occur. Ignore them.

Our personal belief is that the Trump Administration will not cause the great unraveling of the bond market. Instead, capitalism will get a reboot from a President who is his own man; is not beholden to special interests; and has a very practical plan of what needs to get done to improve the quality of life for a majority of Americans.

We believe that the promised reduction in governmental regulation will reinvigorate our economy without the horrific downside feared by the left. Americans and our business leaders are not the greedy, unlawful, takers they were accused of being during the electoral campaign.

We believe that the promised lower corporate tax rate will further stimulate an economy that has been regulated into sluggishness for eight long years. Lastly, we believe that many global corporations will repatriate their offshore cash to the US. Look for them to deploy it into the real economy. This will be additive to our economy's growth.

Focus on just these three signs and act

There are three reasons why we don't believe a wicked, bloody bear market will unravel the credit markets, stock markets, or the economy. They can be summed up as the trifecta:

1. Revamping the tax code
2. Reducing regulations
3. Repatriation of corporate cash

Inflation remains the Darth Vader of the bond market. We believe it will remain tame.

Don't listen to the pundits warning of a bond market cataclysm ahead. They've been saying the same thing for the last nine years and haven't yet been right.

* * *

Best wishes for profitable investing,

Marilyn Cohen & Chris Malburg

About the authors

Marilyn Cohen

Marilyn Cohen is one of the country's top bond managers. She began her 38-year financial career as a securities analyst at William O'Neil & Co. She moved into bond brokerage at Cantor Fitzgerald, Inc. then founded Envision Capital Management 23 years ago. As Envision's CEO, Marilyn and her company specializes in managing bond portfolios for individuals.

During this same 23 years Marilyn has written the bond column appearing in **Forbes** magazine, and has written three books about investing in bonds.

Marilyn is a popular guest on CNBC, Fox Business News, PBS and each of the major broadcast networks. Contact Marilyn at 800.400.0989 or by email at envision@envisioncap.com.

Chris Malburg

Chris Malburg, a product of Stanford Writers School, is a widely published author. With over 4 million words in print scattered among 28 books and over 100 magazine articles, his work is consumed in most western countries. He writes on the subjects of management, business strategies, and financial terrorism (*God's Banker* and *Man of Honor*). He lives in Southern California with his wife where they are volunteer puppy raisers for Canine Companions for Independence (www.cci.org) and Guide Dogs for the Blind (http://www.guidedogs.com).

* * * *

Connect with us online

Marilyn Cohen:
  Website: www.Envision@EnvisionCap.com

Chris Malburg:
  Website: www.WritersResourceGroup.com
  Twitter: http://twitter.com/#!/ChrisMalburg
  Facebook: http://facebook.com/chris.malburg
  Linkedin: http://www.linkedin.com/in/chrismalburg

* * * *

A final word from the authors

We hope you enjoyed *The Great Unravel* and will profit from its lessons. We invite you to enter a review on whatever platform you purchased it. Just log in and give as many stars as you think our effort deserves. Finally, our readers are generous with their emails and tweets. We always make time to answer. If you wish to send us a note, you are welcome to send it to envision@envisioncap.com .

Best wishes,

Marilyn Cohen and Chris Malburg

Other books by Marilyn Cohen and Chris Malburg

The Little Bond eBook
Surviving the Bond Bear Market
Bonds Now!
Bond Bible

About Envision Capital

Minimum account size: $500,000
Annual fees:
    Municipal bonds: .43%
    Investment Grade Corporates: .60%
    Split rated: .75%
    High yield: 1.00%

There are break points in fees depending on account size.
Contact us for further details:
    Telephone: 800.400.0989
    Email: envision@envisioncap.com
    Address: 2301 Rosecrans Ave. Suite 4180
                      El Segundo CA 90245

www.ingramcontent.com/pod-product-compliance
Lightning Source LLC
Chambersburg PA
CBHW070721180526
45167CB00004B/1570